YOUR COMPANION
AFTER **DIVORCE**

CHAPTERS BY NEIL SHARPE
DEVOTIONS BY MANDY MCDOW

OUT OF
THE DEPTHS

Abingdon Press
Nashville

OUT OF THE DEPTHS:
YOUR COMPANION AFTER DIVORCE

Copyright © 2019 by Abingdon Press

This book is printed on acid-free paper.

978-1-5018-8134-3

19 20 21 22 23 24 25 26 27 28—10 9 8 7 6 5 4 3 2 1
MANUFACTURED IN THE UNITED STATES OF AMERICA

CONTENTS

INTRODUCTION

I cry out loud for help from the LORD.
I beg out loud for mercy from the LORD....
When my spirit is weak inside me, you still know my way.
—Psalm 142:1, 3

I f you are reading this booklet, you are either on the cusp of, in the midst of, or have experienced a divorce. This is not what you planned when you got married. You had many dreams, desires, and expectations of how your life would look. You dated, married, and began your life with your spouse, probably never imagining anything could derail the commitment and love you had for each other. Now you have lost your former identity, sense of direction, and vision for the future. Maybe this happened over-night and without warning. Maybe you worked hard to repair the relationship and hold it together only to find nothing was really changing. It may seem that you can do no more than cry, wait, watch, and hope for rescue.

This little book is intended to be a companion in grief. It is organized into two parts. The first is educational. It is our sincere hope that this knowledge will provide a useful framework within which to understand your personal experience of divorce. The second part of the book is devotional and consists of thirty daily scripture readings, and prayers. It is our sincere prayer that these readings lend a sense of connectedness—both to God and to others. You do not have to read the first part of this book before beginning the devotions.

The contents of this book draw from our experiences as care providers.

We have walked with families through the divorce process but found the experience to be quite different when it was Mandy's marriage ending. Her devotions focus on the broad range of feelings encountered in the divorce journey.

If this book has found its way into your hands, you are in the midst of a devastating loss, and for that we are deeply sorry. We have written these words with the prayer that you will know that you are not alone in this terrible grief and are capable of surviving—and even thriving—in spite of it. We are honored to walk with you. Let's begin the journey of healing together.

Blessings and peace,
Neil Sharpe and Mandy McDow

Chapter One

SHATTERED
DREAMS AND HOPES

When I work with a couple in premarital or marriage counseling, I ask each individual to give me some words or phrases that would describe what he or she wants in the marital relationship. I often hear things such as partnership, trust, best friends, family, someone who will love me for me, adventure and travel, safety, and so forth. These are their hopes and dreams for how life could look with their partner. Most of the words my clients offer express a spirit of feeling securely attached to someone.

Research indicates there are three major components that every individual needs to feel secure and satisfied in a marriage relationship: accessibility ("I reach you"), responsiveness ("I can rely on you to respond to me on a healthy emotional level"), and engagement ("You value me and want to stay close"). In other words, these components answer the question "Are you there for me?" No one can meet our needs 100 percent of the time. But what we all want is someone who demonstrates that they can be there for us the majority of the time. When this ability and willingness erodes in one or both individuals, the marital dreams and hopes are shattered. This erosion can be gradual over time or sudden, but in either case, you can feel as though you've been cast into chaos, whatever your role in the decision to divorce.

Someone who is leaving the marriage has usually been thinking about it for some time. There likely has been a gradual erosion of the relationship, progressing from marital dissatisfaction (my needs are not being acknowledged or met), to disaffection (I no longer want physical and emotional support), to disconnection (apathy: I don't care). They may have begun the emotional disconnection process long before their spouse recognized what was occurring. They may have considered moving on to another relationship or just longed for a new start or radical life change. If this is you, your mind is already made up, and you are leaving. You feel the only way to bring order to the chaos you are experiencing is to leave and start over. It is my hope that this book will provide a helpful picture of what the journey ahead holds.

The majority of clients I work with are the individuals who are being left behind and facing divorce reluctantly. If you have been left behind, it may have seemed sudden. Your spouse may have "dropped a bomb" on you. Suddenly all of the hopes, dreams, and plans you had made are scattered and blowing around you. Your spouse may have completely shut down and is no longer willing to communicate with you, or you may have received divorce papers without warning. You may be left in bewilderment and shock. The marital path forward was suddenly washed away. You now find yourself confused and fearful of where and how to go on. If this is you, it is my hope that this book will provide a map to hope and healing.

The end of a marriage means the loss of both what is and what could be. Such a deep loss is wrought with grief, however the decision was reached.

THE STAGES OF GRIEF

The divorce journey is very similar to the five stages of grief outlined by Elisabeth Kubler-Ross. The first stage is *denial*, which is a temporary defense mechanism. You may think or say phrases such as "I feel fine" or "This can't be happening to me." The second stage is *anger*. You may recognize that the denial cannot continue. Many times underneath the anger lurks fear, sadness, hurt, or even embarrassment, but the easier emotion to access at this stage is anger. You may say "Why me?" "It's not fair!" or "Who is to blame (for my pain)?" The third stage is *bargaining*. In this stage you may be trying to return to your "normal." Whether that normal felt healthy or unhealthy, we all want to move back to what we know instead of moving into the unknown. Bargaining sounds like "I will do anything for a few more years," "Let's just wait until the children leave home," or "Maybe they will change if I . . . ." The fourth stage is *depression*. The signs of being in this stage are varied and might include loss of interest or pleasure in your normal activities, weight loss or gain, disturbance in sleeping patterns, physical or mental sluggishness, feelings of worthlessness or guilt, trouble concentrating, or thoughts of suicide. If you have thoughts of harming yourself, please contact your mental or medical care provider immediately, go to the nearest emergency room, or call the suicide prevention line 1-800-784-2433 (or the deaf hotline 1-800-799-4889).

The final stage of grief is *acceptance*. One of the best models for acceptance is the Serenity Prayer, typically attributed to Reinhold Niebuhr (1892–1971):

> God, grant me the serenity
> to accept the things I cannot change,
> courage to change the things I can,
> and wisdom to know the difference.

In acceptance we begin to acknowledge our pain, let go of our ideas of how things "should be," and accept reality—how things really are. At the same time, we discern what we can control and what we cannot. You are gradually moving forward toward a new normal.

THE STATIONS OF DIVORCE

In his book *Divorce and After*, anthropologist Paul Bohannan describes divorce as an intense journey that includes six different stations.[1] You may be facing two or more of these experiences simultaneously. Let's consider each experience briefly.

1. Emotional Divorce. You and your spouse become emotionally distant. You may be functioning on a practical level: caring for children, handling finances, and maintaining your home, but the emotional connection you once had has eroded to the point that you are emotionally shut down. This process happens over time and is mostly felt privately as the marriage weakens. You secretly may have feelings of guilt, anger, or sadness—all of which are a natural reaction to loss.

2. Legal Divorce. This is the legal demise of the relationship. What takes place at this station can be varied. It can be easy or hard, short or long, clean or messy—or anything in between. If you and your spouse mutually decide to dissolve the marriage, you may be able to agree to split everything evenly, devise a plan, and have it legally approved. If that is not the case, some couples use a structured mediation approach with a trained and impartial mediator. The objective of this approach is focused on the quality of the family life by offering the divorcing couple a cooperative method of conflict resolution. The mediator will help create an agreement that includes details about distribution of the marital assets, parenting plans, and so forth. The last stage of this process is often the most emotionally, mentally, and physically challenging: dissolving the marriage through legal representation and action. Frequently, the legal action becomes quite embittered, with lawyers and clients fueling conflicts when emotions are naturally already running very high. You might be wrestling with feeling helpless and out of control as attorneys and courts take over some of your decisions. If you find yourself in this position, remember you are the client and have the ability to direct your attorney's approach after listening to his or her advice.

3. Economic. Even before the legal station of divorce, one or both of the individuals in the marriage may be fearful of experiencing financial stress. Economic divorce generally results in a reduction in standard of living. If one of the spouses did not work for compensation outside of the home, he or she may have to go back to work. Some may have to get further education to find a job that will support their new life. Decisions on where to live and how to financially support children, or even your ex-spouse, are confronting both parties. Individuals who once functioned as a couple now have to learn to function independently.

4. Co-Parental. If you have children, this station can be one of the most emotionally draining. At this station, you and your ex-spouse will determine the rules for custody, visitation rights, and financial support. You may be concerned how the divorce process will affect the children immediately and in the future. You may experience feelings of guilt from seeing your children in pain. Remember one thing during this time: *Your children just want to know that they are still loved, that this isn't their fault, and that they will be okay.* Even though you may not be feeling secure, you can be a secure, safe place for your children.

5. Community. You may find yourself asking, "Where do I fit now?" The support (or lack thereof) from family and friends may be startling. People you thought you could count on don't seem to be as responsive as they were in the past. Your friends and even extended family may appear to be starting to take sides. What is happening? You are experiencing the reactions of the outside world to the breakup. In fact, you may witness different reactions in your social groups, extended family, friendships, and community relationships as you divorce.

If your typical sources for support are coming up short—or even if they're not—look for support from your church staff, a professional counselor, or a divorce support group. Joining a support group can help you feel less isolated by finding others who are on a similar journey. Broadening your support network will be a valuable resource in the future as well.

6. Psychic. At this station you are separating from your ex-spouse emotionally, physically, and mentally. You are separating self from the ex-spouse's personality and influence. You have to break the interdependency or bond. You are now on your own journey, discovering or rediscovering who you are and who you want to be. You are ready to reflect on and learn from your experience. What did you learn from the experience? What do you need to let go of, and what do you keep? Who are you now that you have experienced this event? Success in moving forward will depend on a healthy and thorough self-examination.

EMOTIONAL OVERLOAD: WHERE DID MY ENERGY GO?

In the depths of chaos, your emotions may make you feel "soul-sick," like every negative emotion is conspiring to attack you all at once, including: disappointment in self and others, abandonment, fear, inadequacy, sadness, anger, betrayal, loneliness, and jealousy. Experiencing multiple heightened emotions at one time will zap your energy mentally, physically, and even spiritually. My clients may say something like, "I didn't get out of the house all weekend. I just wanted to lie in bed in the dark. I had no energy."

You may feel you are running very low on faith and hope some days, but there is good news! Over time, the intensity (how strong), duration (how long), and frequency (how often) of these negative emotions will begin to decrease.

After two years of working with a client who moved through her own journey and felt like she was in a better spot, I asked, "As you think back through the past couple of years, how do you see yourself now?" My client thought a bit and said, "It is hard to believe that I could get to a new me, a new normal, and a place of hope. But I finally feel alive again." Someday you will too. Hold on to that hope.

Chapter Two

IDENTITY CRISIS

According to Stephen Covey, our vision and values live at the center of our "circle of influence." Our emotional and personal worth rest there; it is the "lens through which we see the world."[1] It is what is most precious to us. If our spouse or family is at the center, and the center is destroyed, we may lose our sense of who we are—our identity.

Loss, although painful, can bring a sense of clarity of mind and spirit. It is where newness can begin and move us toward answering what we most need at the center of our lives. We realize what is really important and meaningful: God can be our center and can bring order to our chaos.

WHERE AM I, AND HOW DID I GET HERE?

Long-term divorce recovery work involves examining your life up until this point. This takes great courage. It is hard to look into the mirror and take a sober look at how the past may be playing out in the present. You may look at your attachment history, considering your family of origin and what you learned to do to "survive" it, whether you ever felt threatened.

We all learn a certain role to play in our families of origin (that is, the families who raised us) at an early age. These roles result in "coping mechanisms," our answer to everyday interactions with our parents and siblings. Some of us learned to be quiet and disappear, while others became very independent. Some of us learned that performing well will get us acceptance, while others learned to morph into whomever we are in front of. All of these are survival skills, and we carry them into our future relationships.

Since they worked for us in our families of origin, we believe they will work for us in our adult relationships. Although we can honor the fact that these survival skills helped us integrate into our families, employing them now may not be the best strategy.

You may have been using these old ways of relating in your marriage, and it may be time to make a change. Sometimes we must unlearn what we learned and adopt a healthier way of interacting with others. My clients and I usually explore several specific past experiences and then connect the dots from their present to their past. Let's walk through some of these main areas together.

Emotional and Physical Support as a Child: A key question to ask is "Who did you go to when you were a child for emotional and physical support?" While some clients can readily answer this question with examples, other clients, after much thought and discussion, express that they didn't have anyone to go to. For these clients I ask, "How did you cope?" I get answers such as, "I played in my room a lot," "I watched TV by myself," "I read superhero stories," or "I found other families in the neighborhood to hang out with." You may have had a similar childhood. You were looking for whatever might bring you comfort and help you to self-soothe and cope. Often we carry these coping mechanisms into adulthood, including marriage.

Parental Conflict: How did your parents handle conflict? What did you witness as a child? Regardless of the level of conflict in your home, you learned how to deal (or not deal) with conflict in a certain way. The pattern you witnessed was normal to you, and it may have been how you handled conflict with your ex-spouse.

Addiction: Having a parent or sibling with an addiction greatly influences a child's survival or coping skills. In some cases, you may have been the caretaker of the whole family. Or maybe you cleaned up the mess that family member made. Perhaps you avoided the situation altogether, learning to become invisible and stay out of sight until the situation cleared or the family member was gone. Are there ways in which these patterns of coping continued and affected your marriage?

Past Relationship History: Reflecting on past romantic relationships is another helpful way to live and learn. Did you date before your relationship with your ex-spouse? If so, for each relationship ask yourself these questions: How old were you? How long did the relationship last? How did the relationship end? What did you learn about yourself and others from the relationship? As you reflect back you may find patterns of behavior that you are carrying into the present.

Trauma and Loss: Mental health practitioners routinely characterize two forms of trauma: Type A trauma, which is the absence of what you should have received while growing up (emotional and physical support), and Type B trauma, which is the bad things that happened to you (physical abuse, verbal abuse, molestation, rape, prolonged childhood sickness, etc.). Traumatic losses could include the death of a parent, a sibling, a close extended family member, or a friend; it could even include losing your ability to do some activity you loved, such as sports or the arts, due to an injury. All of these events have a profound effect on how we learn to maneuver life and play a part in our present.

Personality: An individual's personality arises from within the individual and remains fairly consistent throughout life. It takes great courage to look back in order to move forward. But it is well worth the effort. By reflecting on how we were designed and how our personality and past experiences shape how we function, we can gain better insight into who we are and how we function within relationships.

Chapter Three

THE PATH FORWARD

We all know the drill. Before a plane takes off, a flight attendant presents a preflight safety briefing pointing out emergency exits. If you are sitting in an exit row, you receive further training about how to facilitate a safe exit for all passengers. The attendants do this because they know that even when everything is crashing down, how you exit makes a difference. When leaving a marriage, you may feel you need to head to the nearest exit to get away from danger. Even so, careful consideration of how you exit may spare you some pain.

In their groundbreaking research, Dr. E. Mavis Hetherington and John Kelly studied fourteen hundred families of divorce over three decades. Hetherington details their findings in *For Better or For Worse: Divorce Reconsidered*. She describes six different ways she observed an individual can exit a marriage. Hetherington states, "Divorce is too complex a process to produce just winners and losers."[1] Let's explore these six ways or roles of exiting a divorce.

The Enhancers: About 20 percent of the individuals (mostly women) chose to create something meaningful out of their setbacks and defeats. They are the Enhancers. These individuals were found to be adaptable and resilient, seizing opportunities and avoiding or overcoming hazards, and improving their life situation through caring and meaningful relationships. They seemed to flourish because of the things that happened to them during and after divorce. Being socially skilled helped them in parenting and often helped in new marriages.

The Competent Loners: About 10 percent of individuals in the study chose not to remarry. They are the Competent Loners. These emotionally self-sustaining individuals did not need or necessarily want a partner. They reported and demonstrated themselves as well-adjusted, self-sufficient, and socially skilled. Many of them had a gratifying career, an active social life, and a wide range of hobbies and interests.

The Good Enoughs: About 40 percent of the individuals said that life after divorce was hard but did not leave a lasting impression—either positive or negative. They are the Good Enoughs. These individuals viewed divorce as a speed bump in the road. They usually remarried, but their post-divorce life often looked a lot like their pre-divorce life.

Shortly after divorce, the Good Enoughs (GEs) started out strong, adapting to the change by attending night school, making new friends, seeking higher-paying jobs, and actively joining new social groups, but they did not have the drive that was characteristic of the Enhancers. Hetherington summarizes that GEs "were muddling through, doing all right at work and at home, but they expressed a certain ill-defined restlessness and yearning for something better in life."[2]

The Seekers: Seekers desired to remarry as quickly as possible. A slightly larger population of this group were men. Seekers often felt rootless and insecure. They needed a spouse in order to have a sense of structure, meaning, and security. Individuals in this group tended to have more drinking problems than other divorced adults. In addition, these individuals went from one "Pursuer-Distancer" marriage—where one spouse is trying to feel closeness and intimacy with the other spouse who considers the pursuit smothering—to another. Finally, Seekers were generally found to neglect children from their first marriage.[3]

The Libertines: Libertines are post-divorce individuals who simply wanted their freedom. Looking to avoid the pain of divorce and seek the freedom that followed, this group had the highest rates of casual sex and spent more time in singles bars. But after a while, these individuals discovered they were unfulfilled and unhappy. Disillusioned, they eventually faced the reality of missing their families and experienced the sadness around their failed marriages.

The Defeated: Individuals in the Defeated group already had problems that worsened after their divorce. Addiction, lack of education, or deficient jobs skills (if their previous spouse had supported them) now left them vulnerable and without the necessary resources to move on in a healthy direction. Some lost everything, while others remained embittered over the life they had lost.

As you can see from the results of this study, there are many ways to exit a marriage. It is my hope that this information will help steer you toward the right exit for you—and any anyone who may be making the journey with you. The next chapter offers help for traveling with children.

OBSTACLES AND HAZARDS

In one episode of *The Simpsons*, Marge warns Homer, her husband, that he may face negative consequences if he doesn't make different choices. Homer says, "That is a problem for future Homer. Man, I don't envy that guy."[1] Like Homer, you are working toward a future you. There are choices that can move us in a healthy direction and other choices that can move us in an unhealthy direction. The obstacles explored below can stand between you and a healthy and vibrant "future you."

There are three sections to the brain: the neocortex (outer), the middle (mammal), and the brain stem (reptilian). Neuroscientists say the youngest part of the brain, in terms of our evolution, is the neocortex. It is responsible for such things as processing the written language, complex thinking, calculating, and rationalizing decisions. The mammal section of the brain processes emotional responses, such as joy, sadness, fear, anger, surprise, and disgust. The oldest part of the brain is the reptilian area. It is responsible for instinct and survival. Its main focus is to *avoid pain*. Our fight, flight, or freeze reactions come from this area. The reptilian brain works great when we need to get out of real danger. But when we experience perceived danger (such as fear of future events based on your past experiences), our brains are wired to move away from that thing that is causing us pain. If we do not analyze the situation with our entire brain but instead simply reach for what feels good, we may make choices that we regret.

The divorce journey can be extremely painful and, given that humans want to avoid pain, we may seek comfort in the following areas.

ROMANTIC RELATIONSHIPS

Loneliness is an extremely painful feeling, and one common to many of my divorced clients. Although seeking close and safe relationships (intimacy) is a healthy response to feeling lonely, moving directly to a romantic and passionate relationship to fill the void can feel good in the short term but delay your healing and perhaps even add to your pain long term. When you find someone you are romantically attracted to, the chemicals phenylethylamine (PEA), norepinephrine, and dopamine are released in the brain. You feel euphoric, your emotional and even physical pain is reduced, and you are essentially "blinded by love." PEA has been found to continue to be released by the brain for up to eighteen months during a romantic relationship. After that time, the "love blindness" wears off, and you become more keenly aware of the stressors of life again: parenting, work, finances, and so forth. Your head-over-heels romantic dreams often tumble to the earth of real life, and you are back where you started. While hope for romance in the future is good and healthy, try not to fall into another relationship prematurely.

ADDICTION

Self-medicating your pain through alcohol, drugs, overeating, gambling, or other harmful activities also stifles healing. Addiction affects the brain's executive functions, therefore eventually affecting your relationships, work or school obligations, and physical health. Specifically, substance abuse has been shown to have a negative impact on emotional maturity. In other words, the escape addicts are seeking stunts their ability to move and mature through the pain, so they remain stuck in time even as they think they are escaping. In the case of divorce adjustment, the addicted individual's judgment is impaired, making it hard to learn from the past, discover a new identity, and heal from past traumas and losses.

SOCIAL ISOLATION

Friends and loved ones provide us with emotional support. Emotional support helps to reduce anxiety and depression when dealing with the pain of divorce. Avoiding opportunities to actively engage in social relationships and gain support can develop into a vicious cycle: more time alone leads to thoughts that people don't understand how you feel and the pain of what you are going through. The less you feel people understand you, the more you want to socially isolate. Make an effort to stay connected, at least to a few close friends. They don't have to share your experience to go through it with you.

Chapter Four

TRAVELING WITH CHILDREN

As I lead divorce adjustment groups, many conversations circle back to the effects on the children. I hear stories of ex-spouses who have abandoned the family either by immersing themselves in another relationship, through addiction, or by completely withdrawing. I hear others tell of an ex-spouse who, when with the children, lavishes them with toys, movies, trips to the amusement park, and other fun events or treats. Still others describe their ex-spouse as an adversary who only wants to use the children to hurt them, using them as pawns in lengthy custody battles, emotional blackmail, and threats. There are many more scenarios, but most parents I see are very concerned about how the divorce will affect their children both in the present and in the future.

Many of my clients have wondered, "Are children from an intact two-parent family better off than my child, who is dealing with the stressors and trials of being in a divorced family?" Much research has been conducted to answer this type of question, yielding different opinions. I have found, though, that research conducted over a long time span (such as the Hetherington and Kelly longitudinal study) provides helpful information about what helps and hurts children during the divorce journey. Specifically, I have found three areas of information helpful to clients when navigating the journey through divorce with children: (1) What challenges will my child have down the road? (2) What can cause harm? and (3) What will help? Let's unpack some of this together.

FUTURE CHALLENGES

I've found that most parents appreciate solid research when it comes to understanding the challenges their children will face as a result of divorce. The Hetherington and Kelly research I referenced in the previous chapter provides some helpful insights gained from a snapshot of the children they were following at the two-year and six-year mark postdivorce.

Two years postdivorce, the researchers found that many children displayed emotional, social, and behavioral problems.[1] Like adults, how well children coped with divorce depended on the stresses they encountered and the personal and social resources they had to rely on. However, the children who improved at the two-year mark did so based on several positive or protective factors:

- the resiliency of children

- moving from a highly conflictual, nonsupportive, or abusive situation before divorce into a safe home environment with a competent custodial parent after the divorce

- living with a caring, competent custodial parent

- parenting that is loving, firm, and consistent

- low conflict between divorced parents

- parents who worked to improve their parenting skills (Note that parenting skills that declined in the first year after a divorce improved the second and third years, perhaps indicating that as the parents adjusted, their parenting improved.)

- having a noncustodial parent who was involved, dependable, and engaged

Overall, they concluded that "an involved, competent custodial parent was the most effective buffer a young child could have against postdivorce stress."[2]

The study also found that the following risk factors hindered children from improving:

- poor parenting practices by the custodial parent, which contributed to poor academic achievement, internalizing and externalizing problems, poor self-esteem, and social incompetence

- depression in the custodial mother

- hostility and lack of cooperation between parents

- lack of social support from friends and relatives

- the noncustodial parent being unreliable and untrustworthy

Overall, they concluded that living with "an irritable, punitive, uncaring, or disengaged parent put the child at great risk for developing problems."[3]

The Hetherington and Kelly study found that by the sixth year after the family's divorce, it was the current stresses and resources, rather than the ones that had surrounded the divorce, that were now most important.[4] The cloud of anxiety and depression that hung over children in the first year had usually diminished or evaporated by the sixth year.

Children in the study tended to follow one of these basic adjustment patterns:

- *Competent-Opportunist*: curious, socially skilled, and charming with a wide range of interests, yet manipulative; generally come from high-conflict parents

- *Competent-Caring*: sensitive and responsive to the feelings and needs of others; generally come from low-conflict parents

- *Competent-at-a-Cost*: remarkably able, successful, and likable but with a lurking sense of anxiety and inadequacy

- *Aggressive-Insecure*: focused on abandonment, not failure

- *Good Enough*: average level of functioning, including 60 percent of post-divorce children

Research on the effect of divorce on children clearly shows that the parents' ability and willingness to engage with their children and foster secure attachments has a dramatic influence on the child's ability to adjust. Exactly what that sort of parenting looks like is worth considering.

PARENTING STYLES THAT HELP AND HURT

First, it can be helpful to understand the four different parenting styles: *authoritative* (which is ideal), *authoritarian*, *permissive*, and *disengaged and neglecting*. As you look at each style, evaluate not only your parenting style but also which one best describes how you were parented.

Disengaged and Neglecting: This parenting style is the most harmful to a child. A neglectful parent doesn't care for the child's emotional and physical needs; doesn't know or care about what is going on in their child's life; spends long periods of time away from home, either leaving the child at home alone or placing the child with anyone available; and chooses not to engage in any activities associated with the child. In this environment, the child has no safe place to return to and no foundation on which to build trust. As a result, the child will have a harder time forming relationships with other people. When I counsel with adults who have had this type of childhood, I categorize it as *developmental trauma* that is the result of chronic abuse, neglect, or other harsh adversity in the child's own home.

Permissive: A permissive parenting style may result in an immature and aggressive child, teen, and adult. This style is also known as the *indulgent parent* who wants to avoid confrontation. This parenting style is deceptively warm and uncontrolling. The parent either wants the child to be his or her friend or just provides food, shelter, and clothing without really focusing on guiding, teaching, or even connecting with the child on an emotional level. Permissive parenting is less controlling, with an insecure reliability to influence the child. It is a weak model that demands little of the child, provides little reinforcement in the way of consequences, enables the child's bad behavior, is less intensely involved with the child, and may use love manipulatively.

Authoritarian: An authoritarian parenting style can produce an anxious (fear-based) and withdrawn child. Specifically, the child may be generally less content, more insecure and apprehensive about exploring, and prone to react (depending on the child's temperament or learned behavior) with a fight, flight, or freeze response when under pressure. This type of parenting is generally described as cold and controlling. Authoritarian parents are less nurturing and involved with children, have rigid or firm control, use power freely but offer little support or affection, have a "Do as I say" mentality, and discourage children from expressing themselves when the parent disagrees.

Authoritative: An authoritative parenting style is generally considered to be the most effective and beneficial parenting style for most children. This is the best style to help your child become self-reliant, self-controlled, content, and curious. This type of parenting is warm but still in control and demonstrates structure; consistency; loving, conscientious, secure, reasonable expectations with direction and reasonable support; firm control;

established consequences; and supportive, open communication. Of the four parenting styles, this one has the best possible outcome for a child. But what does the authoritative style look like, and how do you stick to it day in and day out—especially under the stressors that divorce has placed on your family?

GOOD PARENTING BEGINS WITH THE END IN MIND

By beginning with the end in mind, we develop a vision and clarity about how we would like to see our children develop and look in the future. This is very powerful. When we begin with the end in mind, we might vision our child as someone who explores, has the ability to self-soothe when emotionally distraught, has self-control, has a positive sense of self, has the ability to face adversity and move through it, and can be content in life whether things are going good or bad. Although we cannot guarantee this outcome, we still need a destination to move toward. Imagine this vision serving like the rudder of a sailboat that helps you steer toward the destination. Just like sailing on the water, you will encounter many factors that will work against your making it toward your destination. But beginning with the end in mind will give you a focal point and allow you to help your child develop in a positive direction.

So how can you support the vision? You become the rudder. You do this by allowing your children to explore. If they encounter threats or obstacles while exploring, we as parents should be the safe harbor our child can return to. When they return, it will give us the opportunity to calm and soothe them emotionally, then help guide and teach them ways to handle the situation in the future. For young children, we are more hands-on and directive. For older children, we become more of a sounding board and counselor, letting them struggle through how to handle the situation—consequences and all.

I want to emphasize that even though you have a vision and are the rudder, your child may still stray from the charted course. Connect first with your child so that you become a safe place, and empower your child to make their own decisions. If you have connected well, they will most likely return to you for correction, but you can't make a child develop as you wish.

PARENTING *DOS* AND *DON'T*S

Whether you are a co-parent (where the children reside in each parent's home part of the time), the custodial parent (with whom the child resides all or most of the time), or the noncustodial parent (the out-of-home parent), certain practices can increase your child's odds of a healthy adjustment.

- Try to keep a routine that the children can follow.

- Assure the children that they are safe and will not be abandoned. Your child is constantly checking, either silently or aloud: Are you there for me? Can I count on you?

- Take care of yourself when the children are with the other parent. In other words, self-care (rest, socialization, exercise, etc.) is very important.

- Expect that children will have some emotional reaction to the new circumstances.

- Do not overindulge the children when they are with you.

- Utilize good communication skills such as empathetic listening and asking nonprying, genuine questions. Do not interrogate your child to get information about your former spouse.

- Create a homelike atmosphere for the children in both homes if you share custody.

- Be very careful before introducing any romantic involvements. If the relationship does not work out, your children will experience another loss.

- Keep your word, and be on time to pick them up. Remember, with each time you show up as planned, you are building a foundation of trust with your child.

- Make sure the children know they are not to blame.

- Do not bicker with your former spouse where the children can see or hear you.

- Keep the children informed, and answer their questions in age-appropriate ways.

- Refrain from making negative comments about the other parent, which can negatively affect the child's self-image. They are, after all, 50 percent the other parent.

Chapter Five

SURVIVOR'S TOOL KIT

H ow can you actively work toward your healing? Clinical psychologist and author Stephen Ilardi outlines six steps that can help reduce or even ward off depression, so often associated with divorce.[1] Consider these six steps as actions you can take as a first line of defense to fight or ward off depression and emerge renewed.

1. Diet: A good diet is always helpful to our overall health. Eating healthy if you are on the go with children or working many hours is difficult, and our society teaches people to turn to food as a source of comfort. Try to eat a variety of foods representing all food groups over the course of the day. Food is the fuel your body, brain, and heart need to grieve, heal, and grow.

2. Engaging Activity: According to Ilardi, "Depression is closely linked to a toxic thought process called *rumination*—the habit of dwelling on negative thoughts, turning them over and over in your mind."[2] Ruminating often happens when we are socially isolated or have a lot of free time on our hands. Ilardi recommends being involved in an "engaging activity" where your mind doesn't have time to dwell on negative thoughts. Picking up a new hobby or joining a new activity could be particularly helpful.

3. Physical Exercise: The antidepressant effect of exercise is well-documented. Ilardi states simply that "exercise changes the brain."[3] It increases the activity level of dopamine and serotonin and the production of a key growth hormone called BDNF. Exercising only three times a week for thirty minutes each time is enough to help protect the brain. Of course, any exercise program should be discussed with your physician to ensure it is and remains appropriate for you specifically.

4. Sunlight Exposure: Sunlight increases vitamin D in your body (which aids in bone and heart health) and benefits mood by increasing serotonin and dopamine levels. Further, as Ilardi explains, "without light exposure, the body clock eventually gets out of sync...throw[ing] off important circadian rhythms that regulate energy, sleep, appetite, and hormone levels. The disruption of these important biological rhythms can, in turn, trigger clinical depression."[4] So, if you see the sun, go join it for a little while!

5. Social Support Network: God designed us for relationship, and we do not do well without it. I can't state enough how important it is that you find social support. I highly recommend joining a divorce support group or finding a counselor to walk with you personally through the divorce adjustment journey. Try to join groups that share your interests or hobbies. Get involved in community service or with serving at your church. Lean on your friends and family to discuss big decisions and issues. Vent your frustrations and share your joys.

6. Sleep: In *Why We Sleep: Unlocking the Power of Sleep and Dreams*, Matthew Walker describes the harmful effects of a lack of regular sleep. Sleeping less than six or seven hours a night breaks down the immune system and poses other health risks.[5] To help you get a full night of sleep, turn off electronics, allow a "wind down" period before bed, and go to bed early.

These six steps are critical to your self-care on the journey to healing.

DEVELOP A FINANCIAL PLAN

Tending to your emotional and psychological health post-divorce is important, as is the case in any kind of trauma. Divorce often brings with it another kind of challenge: financial instability. No matter your circumstance, the shape, size, and structure of your financial situation is likely to be affected by divorce. If you weren't very involved with the money management of your household before your divorce, you may be particularly challenged in this area and tempted to neglect it. Unfortunately, though, the more you avoid something, the bigger it grows. When you face your financial reality head-on, you may find that it is not the monster you imagined.

First, take a sober look at all of your financial needs and the resources that can help meet those needs. Even though looking at your financial health can be overwhelming to some, make sure you don't avoid this task. If you have never put together a budget, you can ask for help from someone who has, and he or she can help you get a realistic view of what you have and what you need financially. Second, after you establish a budget, be vigilant about tracking expenses. If you do, you can minimize the *uh-oh* moments that can possibly throw you into a financial tailspin. Finally, make a plan to improve your financial situation, if necessary. At first, think of ways to use your current talents to earn income. Eventually, you may seek new skills through further education or skill development.

Taken together, these suggestions can be your survivor's tool kit. Even if you feel like your divorce is happening *to* you, utilizing your tool kit can help you make sense of the chaos and begin to ascend from the depths.

ARRIVING AT YOUR DESTINATION

In the first year following divorce, you (and your children) may feel pain, confusion, emptiness, disorientation, or disillusionment. You will encounter many "firsts"—the first holidays, birthdays, and anniversaries as a divorced person. You may hear that your ex-spouse is in a new relationship or view posts on social media from or about your ex-spouse that make you want to tear your hair out. You many want comfort—and want it now! Year one is hard.

But hold on. Year two is coming, and Hetherington and Kelly's research says that "life" starts to emerge from the ground after the first year for those who take their advice.[1] First, view your divorce as an opportunity to personally grow and build enhanced, new, and more fulfilling relationships. Second, in the first year of divorce, be very careful about the choices you make because many of them can last a lifetime. Third, after you have reflected on how you got to this place in life, set your sights toward the future by developing priorities and goals. These goals are personal and can be around meaningful and purposeful life experiences through work and relationships. Fourth, take an inventory and capitalize on your personal strengths and the resources you have available to you. Fifth, roll with the inevitable bumps and detours; learn from them and discover how resilient you can be.

Eventually, you will begin to accept what happened, reorganize your life, and recover. Acceptance doesn't mean that when you think about it you will not feel some sadness or hurt; instead, it means the sadness or hurt will not overwhelm you when it resurfaces. In time, you will emerge from these depths transformed.

COVENANT

Out of the depths I cry to you, LORD. Lord, hear my voice.
Let your ears be attentive to my cry for mercy.
—Psalm 130:1-2 (NIV)

The first night alone in a bed made for two, knowing that the circumstances weren't temporary, was bleak. No good marriage ends, and when the truth of its end hits, a swirl of mixed emotions finally surfaces. Perhaps relief floods your senses, and guilt soon after. It seems wrong to feel peace about the curtain being torn, the covenant being broken. What once anchored you in your life—your spouse, your children—is no longer the first consideration.

Psalm 130 is a psalm of disorientation. Biblical scholar Walter Brueggemann says Psalm 130 is "the miserable cry of a nobody from nowhere."[1] It feels as though this is the experience of divorce: there is no longer the tested covenant relationship in which we can voice our laments and praises. Now, our voices go unheard because our partner has gone. The safe place to voice concerns, joys, sorrows, anxieties is no longer in the presence of your most intimate partner. The psalmist reminds us that we have a covenant relationship with our creator, who promised to be with us, always. Even if our earthly covenants have been broken, God offers the model of a relationship that will stand the depths of pain, despair, and anger. God shows us what it means to be faithful, so that we can practice covenant with the eternal presence who loved us first and best.

◇◇

Abiding and Incarnate God, hear my voice. Consider my prayers.
I am in the depths of despair and loss and pray for your Holy Spirit
to encircle me with peace, that I may not feel so alone.
Abide with me, even in the depths. Amen.

◇◇

CONFESSION

If you, LORD, kept a record of sins, Lord, who could stand?
—Psalm 130:3 (NIV)

The hardest part of coming to the end of a relationship is recognizing the mutuality of failing. Sometimes the end is defined by an event, a choice, or a shift in perspective. It is very easy to defend your heart and its sensitivities, and no healthy relationship is without flaws or issues.

You are now redefining your relationship with your spouse, and both of you need to hear the same thing: "I'm sorry for what I have done and what I have left undone." You may not fully understand the scope of your spouse's complaints, nor may your spouse understand yours. Own the expectations that your spouse held for you that you could not meet. Own the expectations you held for your spouse that also couldn't be met. The rift that could not be healed is bound in your mutual unmet expectations. Now, you are free of them.

We are all imperfectly striving to love God and one another, and yet, we fail. This doesn't mean that *you* are a failure; it means that your marriage was an imperfect fit. Give your marriage, your failings, your woes, and your brokenness back to God. Ask for your spouse's forgiveness, if you are ready, and confess your faults. This act may not be reciprocated, just like many of your broken expectations. Be at peace with who you are, broken and flawed. God made you and loves you in all of it.

◇◇◇◇◇◇◇◇◇◇◇◇◇◇◇◇◇◇◇◇◇◇◇◇◇◇◇◇◇◇◇◇◇◇◇◇◇

Holy and Loving God, I confess that I have made mistakes,
even if I can't identify them yet. Soften my heart to hear
the confession of my spouse in words or actions,
so that we may be free from our broken relationship. Amen.

◇◇◇◇◇◇◇◇◇◇◇◇◇◇◇◇◇◇◇◇◇◇◇◇◇◇◇◇◇◇◇◇◇◇◇◇◇

FORGIVENESS

But forgiveness is with you—
that's why you are honored.

—*Psalm 130:4*

If forgiveness were easy, the world would be a more peaceful place. But forgiveness is hard. If you are having trouble asking for forgiveness, and offering it to your spouse, start with what you need God to forgive *you*. In the Lord's Prayer, Jesus taught his disciples to say, "Forgive us our debts, as we forgive our debtors" (Matthew 6:9-13 KJV). Forgiveness is a two-way street; it is a conditional relationship.

God's forgiveness is a gift to us, given, not earned. But, it is important to realize that God expects us to forgive others just as much as we hope to be forgiven by God. Forgiveness is an exercise in letting go, releasing your heart from the bitterness and anger that it has collected, and pursuing the freedom of an unbound future. Your life will change, your finances will change, your address may change. God's promise to forgive you, just as you forgive others, will not.

Perhaps the hardest direction of forgiveness will be toward yourself. The litany of things you could have, should have, or wish to have done is endless. The first step of forgiving yourself is to name these things to God, and offer them with humility. Be honest with what was possible and what was impossible; certain things cannot be changed, including who you are. God intends for us to be as God made us.

◇◇

Gracious and Loving Lord, in you, there is forgiveness.
All I need to do is ask. Help me to find the courage to be honest
about my failings, own them, and address them.
Forgive me, and help me to forgive my spouse,
that we may learn to live in peace. Amen.

◇◇

LONELINESS

I wait for the LORD, my whole being waits,
and in his word I put my hope.

—*Psalm 130:5 (NIV)*

While making myself dinner one night, I reached for a plate that my spouse and I had chosen when we registered for wedding gifts. These plates had been the bearers of meals for us when we had no knowledge of how to prepare food, meals for our infant children when we had no clue how to parent, meals for our guests when we joyfully welcomed them into our home. These plates were more than plates. These plates were the symbols of a common table, shared experiences, time's passing. I felt the feeling that was growing all-too familiar: a stabbing pain in my heart as the reality of my aloneness took hold. I slowly began to realize that I had a new life-partner: Loneliness.

When I awoke on days without children in the house, it was Loneliness who walked me to the kitchen to make the coffee. When I arrived home in the evening after a long meeting, it was Loneliness who met me at the door. When I thought about what I would do with an unscheduled day, it was Loneliness who texted first to check in on my availability. The truth is, Loneliness is always available. Loneliness is the sibling of Depression, and they will show up, uninvited, and overstay their welcome. I struggled with how to break things off with Loneliness. In the midst of a fist-shaking prayer to God, the resounding answer came, a deep awareness of God's abiding presence with me: "I am here, dear one. You are never alone."

Holy and Ever-Present God,
help me to remember that you love me
and that you are always with me.
You, alone, are enough. Amen.

GRIEF

My whole being waits for my Lord—
more than the night watch waits for morning.

—*Psalm 130:6*

Like the rising tide of an ocean, the waves of grief will lap at you at unexpected intervals. Some days will pass with peace and calm. Other days, the grief will rage with a ferocity unknown before. The darkest nights of your soul will bring the feeling that you will never get over this.

When a relationship ends, you have typically seen signs that the tapestry of your life together is coming unwoven. But there are ways in which a marriage ending is something you cannot fully comprehend. It was as if my spouse had died, but only to me. My grief couldn't even be shared, because no one else experienced it as I did. There are ways in which your life will never look the same after divorce. This is more than a break-up; it is a covenant's end, and, as with any loss, it takes time for the light to shine brighter again.

Even so, believe what God promises: it is *worth* watching for the morning. One day, when you least expect it, something new will happen. This might be a job opportunity you never could have accepted in your marriage. It might be the chance to take on a new hobby and meet new friends. It might be meeting the person with whom you will build a new and different life. Your chance at love—whether romantic or platonic—isn't over. This is what God promises to us in resurrection: that death doesn't have the last word. This is true for your life, especially now. Joy will come in the morning.

Holy and Loving God, help me to heal from my grief,
and to perpetually seek the light that shines in the darkness,
for the darkness did not overcome it. Amen.

TIME

Israel, wait for the Lord!
Because faithful love is with the Lord;
Because great redemption is with our God!
He is the one who will redeem Israel from all its sin.

—Psalm 130:6

After years of disappointment, Hannah finally gave birth to a child, Samuel. As promised, Hannah gave Samuel back to the Lord by allowing him to be raised in the temple by the priest, Eli. I wonder how Hannah did it. Her prayed-for, beautiful wonder, the child of her fidelity to God, was left in the care of a priest whose own children had turned their backs on God and their father.

What were those first days like for Hannah, returning to her home, her body, the quiet. Perhaps she is better than I am in accepting that nothing is truly ever ours, and that what God gives, God can take away. She knew from the beginning that Samuel's life would be given away. But, I can't help but think that her heart didn't stop its longing for the milk-drunk sleep smiles or chubby-fisted grabs at her hair.

On the days that the house is filled with quiet, and the unmade beds don't have knobby knees returning to them at the end of the day, my heart is so broken it can hardly afford to beat. This is particularly true on the first day the children are away; the clamor, demands, and chaos give way to a definitive quiet that is less restorative than it is mockery. I pray to have the peace of Hannah, whose faithfulness gave her both the child of prayers and the depth of understanding that he is hers, no matter where his head lies to rest.

Almighty Creator, you are with us, whether we are near or far from you.
Remind us that the same is true with our children,
for love knows no bounds. Amen.

INDIVIDUALITY

You have searched me, Lord,
and you know me.

—*Psalm 139:1 (NIV)*

Being fully known by someone takes time and devotion. In a marriage, you have invested much of yourself and your care into someone else, getting to know and love him or her and inviting the same toward you. Your spouse becomes a part of your identity, your family, your story. When a marriage ends, it shifts the course of your future in ways that you did not anticipate when you made promises before God and these witnesses. No longer can you assume that you will have a partner in all things. The person who knew you best will no longer be a part of your daily life. This is hard. But also, this is okay.

You have already been searched and known by the creator of heaven and earth. You are known more fully by God than you realize. It is hard to think of your life as an individual when you have been orienting your thoughts around another person. Understanding that God knows you, with all of your flaws, failings, and beauty, will help you live into your identity as an individual who is, now and always, worthy of love. The investment you spent searching and knowing your spouse was not lost. The experience of being searched and known by another was not wasted. This sort of vulnerability has shaped you into the person that God always knew you to be.

Holy and Loving God, you have searched me and known me.
You have cared for me and guided my steps.
Help me, now, as I discover who I am as an individual,
to love myself on my own terms,
just as you have always loved me. Amen.

INTIMACY

You know when I sit down and when I stand up.
Even from far away, you comprehend my plans.
—*Psalm 139:2*

The psalmist writes about being known and cared for enough that God knows when he sits down and when he stands up. This kind of intimacy is rare and precious. Perhaps there was a time when you and your spouse could know what the other was thinking. Divorce means a loss of this sort of closeness and intimacy. There is a beauty in human contact that cannot be easily replicated.

Take comfort in knowing that your spouse was not the only one to know you this well. Before you ever met, God created you with such love and devotion that God knew your rhythms, preferences, and hopes. God understood your thoughts and longings, even more so than any lover could. God loves you so much that God refused to stay distant from us, and became flesh and blood in the person of Jesus.

There will be days when you miss the personal contact of your spouse, and that touch can feel irreplaceable. Still, God became incarnate—one of us—so that we might not experience anything in isolation. There were times when Jesus withdrew to be alone, and there were times when Jesus relished the comfort of Mary anointing his feet. Jesus shared his very self with us, offering us grace and connection to the Divine through the bread and wine of communion. There are a myriad of healthy ways to honor and seek out intimacy; doing so is as sacred as prayer.

Loving and Incarnate God, help me
to discover intimacy that mirrors the love you offer to us.
Show me comfort and care that seeks to give
as much as it receives. Amen.

SEPARATION

You study by traveling and resting.
You are thoroughly familiar with all my ways.
—*Psalm 139:3*

No one gets married with the idea that he or she will get divorced. When you marry, you agreed that each of you can be your best self with and to the other. But even in the best of marriages, people become their worst selves at times. It is also true that your worst self could be brought out by your spouse; this doesn't mean that you are bad people, it simply means that you are not your best selves together. Agreeing to separate is challenging, and this is not the path you could have anticipated when you got married.

The beauty of your life is that God searches out your path. This doesn't mean that God knew you would marry a partner who would not be in your life forever. Rather, it means that no matter where your path leads, God will be with you. Your path is taking a sharp turn in a direction you didn't anticipate. You will be faced with the challenge of separating your life, possessions, time, and money. The legal process is painful and tedious. Be reassured that God is with you and your spouse on this pathway that will lead to new life for each of you. God is acquainted with all of your ways and will guide you both down your separate paths.

Holy and Discerning God, guide me on my new path;
give me peace, grace, and forgiveness as I go.
Help me understand that the path I am on
will lead me in the right direction,
even if this journey looks different than I'd planned. Amen.

MEMORY

There isn't a word on my tongue, Lord,
that you don't already know completely.

—*Psalm 139:4*

After a divorce, your memories will evoke very different feelings than they once did. Memories that were painted with a patina of soft gold will now begin to tarnish. What once brought you joy now brings you pain. There are small things that you can do to ease some of the pain around your memory, though you cannot avoid the feelings altogether. If a particular memory of an event or place is pressing on you, tell it to God. Talk through what you remember; use your words to describe the time, place, circumstance. God knows what is in your heart: all of the complicated, conflicting emotions around your memories are just as tender to God as they are to you.

In a divorce, it's natural to carry anger and disappointment toward your spouse. You will be asked, again and again, the story of your separation. Though it is tempting to take this chance to harm your spouse through your words, be as kind and fair as you can be; speak honestly and directly about your experiences. If you have children, consider how you speak of their other parent. God understands how painful this experience is for you. Soften your words, guard your heart, and let your memories be a blessing to you.

Holy and Gracious God, incline your ear to the words of my heart.
Hear, with grace, my words of pain and regret. Listen with kindness
to my prayers for peace and forgiveness. Help me to use my words
for good, that I may speak of my memories and my spouse
with compassion. Amen.

ISOLATION

You hem me in behind and before,
and you lay your hand upon me.

—Psalm 139:5 (NIV)

As I divorced, I changed my insurance plan and had to choose a new doctor. The typical new patient form is filled with questions about intimate, personal details of your life and health. It is also an unexpected place to be prompted into tears, as normally this form is filled with little effort. At my first office visit, though, my pen hovered over the place where my spouse's name would normally be written as The Emergency Contact. It was so jarring to be left with the absence of the go-to person who would respond in case something happened. My heart skipped beats as I blinked back tears. "Does anyone care now?" The blank on the form, in the absence of a default person, begged the question.

The psalmist's words remind us that we are never alone, even in the depths of loss and rediscovery. There is comfort in knowing that God holds us carefully, so that nothing in our past or our future can separate us from the love that we are given. Breathe, exhale, and remember that you are created, not just for partnership, but for the ways in which your unique spirit has changed the world. Consider the people whose lives would be altered if something happened to you. Think of the friends who you might also need an emergency contact and offer to be their go-to first call. This is not simply a loss; it can be an opportunity to expand your circle of care and compassion.

Holy and Loving God,
help me to remember that I am yours,
you hold me fast,
and you will never let me go. Amen.

REDISCOVERY

Such knowledge is too wonderful for me,
too lofty for me to attain.

—Psalm 139:6 (NIV)

As a married person, much of your life has been devoted to negotiations of some sort. You made decisions for two people, often without even realizing it. Now, your life will be different. You have the opportunity to make decisions for yourself, without making concessions on someone else's behalf. If you're like me, the gift of being without the limits of another person is often overwhelmed by the terrifying vastness of possibility. Sometimes parameters are comfortable!

You have the opportunity now to rediscover yourself, in light of and because of your marriage. Living in covenant relationship with another has changed you, shaped you, and formed you in a particular way. Take some time to give thanks for the person that you are, all by yourself. Give thanks for the people who have loved you and cared for you; they have shaped you into the person you are today. Now, let your mind wander. Let your imagination run wild. Allow yourself to be bored. God knows what your heart longs for now; God holds you in this liminal time and can see what good lies in store for you. Take time to enjoy getting to know yourself all over again: the person you are now is interesting, beautiful, and resilient. What an amazing thing it is to be you!

Almighty and Creative God,
help me as I begin to rediscover myself,
learning about who I am
and who you have always known me to be.
I want to enjoy being me for me. Amen.

RELIEF

Where could I go to get away from your spirit?
Where could I go to escape your presence?

—*Psalm 139:7*

t is commonly said that no good marriage ends in divorce. When it comes time to share the news publicly of your separation from your spouse, you get a number of responses. Most people will offer sympathy in recognition of your loss. But if your marriage had come to its end, you may feel a strange sense of relief. You are now free from the arguing and disappointment, the failed expectations and mutual woes. Separating means facing the unknown instead of what was known, which was too painful to endure any longer.

There is profound relief in knowing that when the difficult decision to let your marriage go is made, you're not fleeing from the presence of God. Psalm 139 reassures us that even in the depths of our despair, shame, or sorrow, we cannot escape the persistent presence of God, who loves us during our most challenging times. There is nowhere you can go that God will leave you abandoned; God sees you, loves you, and will guide you and your spouse into the hopeful space of gratitude for your marriage. You have the ability to choose peace. May your relief be a welcome sign of all that is to come.

Holy and Merciful God, I am relieved to know
that wherever life takes me, you are there.
Some days, I feel far from you.
Remind me that I cannot wander so far
away that you are not with me.
Grant me peace and sweet relief
from the battles that waged,
which could not be won. Amen.

FAMILY

If I went up to heaven, you would be there.
If I went down to the grave, you would be there too!
—Psalm 139:8

On my first Mother's Day after the divorce, I found myself jarred by the longstanding tradition around this day. I did what we had always done, which was make reservations at a restaurant that served brunch, and dragged my church-weary kids to a packed venue with inflated prices. I ordered for the kids and myself, and unceremoniously paid the bill. The lack of an accompanying spouse at our table seemed to highlight the seas of intact family units sitting all around us, toasting the matriarch for her care and sacrificial love. I left feeling embarrassed and defeated (not to mention broke). I felt like my claims to family were just as broken as my vows.

In our wedding ceremony, we acknowledge that our marriage unites two families and creates a new one. You have the gift of the family who raised you, and the family who raised your spouse. Even if you and your spouse do not form a family unit any longer, your understanding of family can broaden. Nothing can change our relationship to our creator, for we are all children of God. What a blessing to know that it is God who defines our family, for we are considered siblings in Christ! Your relationship with your former spouse and in-laws will change and shift, but your relationship with God will persist. God reassures us that no matter what our family structure looks like, God will be present with us.

◇◇◇◇◇◇◇◇◇◇◇◇◇◇◇◇◇◇◇◇◇◇◇◇◇◇◇◇◇◇◇◇◇◇◇◇◇

Holy and Loving God, I take comfort in knowing
that you are with me in the best of times and the worst of times.
Thank you for coming to the world in the person of Christ
to create a Holy Family, of which I am always a part. Amen.

◇◇◇◇◇◇◇◇◇◇◇◇◇◇◇◇◇◇◇◇◇◇◇◇◇◇◇◇◇◇◇◇◇◇◇◇◇

SIN

If I could fly on the wings of dawn,
stopping to rest only on the far side of the ocean—
even there your hand would guide me;
even there your strong hand would hold me tight!
                                    —Psalm 139:9-10

One of the hardest things to come to terms with in a separation is that you have also wronged your spouse. No person, or spouse, is perfect. Each party has complaints about the other, and each person is entitled to his or her perspective on the marriage and what went wrong. There will be times, both in your marriage and in the ensuing disentanglement from it, that you will be tempted to think and say terrible things about your spouse. The psalmist writes about our inclination to fly fast to the farthest limits of the sea, where it feels as though we will be distanced from the reality of our circumstances. In these dark places, it is tempting to let your anger overwhelm your spirit.

Feelings of anger will almost certainly surface during your divorce, and managing how you communicate it is critical. Most of us will turn to the legal system to process our anger and seek justice for the wrongs that have befallen us. But, remember, while anger is a perfectly legitimate feeling, expressing it inappropriately can be destructive, both to you and those around you. Do your best to feel your anger without letting it overtake you. Don't deny your anger, but don't let anger guide your decisions. Remember that God offers you grace for your sins and invites you to do the same for your spouse.

Holy and Merciful God, hear my prayer.
Sometimes, my anger overtakes me and affects my thinking.
Clear my thoughts. Help me to confess my sins to you,
to own what I have done
to contribute to my relationship's end.
Help me, even more, to forgive my spouse
for the hurt and disappointment. Amen.

VOWS

...your hand would guide me;
even there your strong hand would hold me tight!
—Psalm 139:10

A copy of our wedding vows used to hang on our wall. Each day, I read the words: "Will you love, comfort, honor, and keep the other, in sickness and in health, and, forsaking all others, be faithful to one another as long as you both shall live?" These vows are simple; they aren't flowery or elegant. They are the barest bones of covenant. Feelings of guilt cutting short a life-long covenant are common in divorcing families. Knowing that one or both of you has come to the end of these promises is painful. Broken vows hurt.

Repeatedly in scripture, God reminds the Israelites of God's faithfulness to them, despite their own failing in the relationship. God relentlessly keeps God's covenant with Abraham, Isaac, Moses, and all of the generations who follow. God keeps God's promises to us, even when we don't keep our promises to God or to each other.

As you separate, you will redefine your relationship with each other. In some cases, you may cease to be in contact. In others, especially if you share children, you will be in an ongoing relationship with your former spouse. How can you behave in such a way that is life-giving to everyone involved? You have the power to continue to love, honor, and care for your spouse in a new way, whether up close and personal or from a significant distance. Your life in a household may be ending, but you might find it easier to get along as a result.

Holy and Faithful God, you have shown me
how to be faithful
in the face of faithlessness.
Help me learn from your example
of supporting each other, even when
the nature of our marital relationship changed. Amen.

DEPRESSION

If I said, "The darkness will definitely hide me;
the light will become night around me,"
even then the darkness isn't too dark for you!
—Psalm 139:11-12

While the beginning of a marriage is usually very public, its end tends to be very private. You choose carefully how and when to tell people the news, and your ability to do so will come in waves. Announcing your change in marital status is a burden, that can weigh heavily on you. For many people, it can be a trigger for their ever-creeping depression.

As you divorce, you may feel as though darkness is covering you, and even the light around you loses its power. Depression is a real and powerful force, and the circumstances before, during, and after a divorce are ripe for the darkness to take hold of your heart. Depression is also a very convincing liar. Depression will tell you that you are worthless, unlovable, and destined for a life of sorrow.

Depression is wrong.

Try to take hold of this force before it does its greatest harm by praying for God's light to shine brighter than the deepest darkness. Reach out to those who care for you, find a counselor, seek out support, talk to your doctor. Even though it is private, you do not have to go through your divorce alone. God knows how painful this experience can be for you, and will not leave you abandoned in the dark. You are claimed as one of God's beloved children, and nothing—not even depression—gets to rob you of this identity.

Holy and Loving God, I can claim the power to fight the darkness.
Send me the people, resources, and help I need to stand strong in the
face of Depression, and remind me that I am always yours. Amen.

HOPE

The darkness isn't too dark for you.
Nighttime would shine bright as day,
because darkness is the same as light to you!

—Psalm 139:12

Even in the most civil of divorces, the process of separating your life from another's is painful. The weight of what you are losing and what will change is heavy. Even in the midst of the overwhelming darkness, a speck of light shines: hope. Hope is not wishing for that which cannot be; it is easy to ask for a different set of circumstances altogether. Hope, rather, is the understanding that God knows more of your future than you can possibly see. This is why the darkness is not dark to God, and even the night can be bright as day.

Hope is possible when we hold to the truth that God is good and works for our good as well. If your marriage has failed, it wasn't a good marriage, at least at its end. It is possible to hope for a future that is better than your past experiences. This doesn't mean that the pain you're enduring is frivolous; it simply means that the worst thing is not the last thing. As poet Jane Hirshfield writes, "Hope is the hardest / love we carry."[2] To hope means to believe that you will continue to find joy, love, and delight in your life. Let your hope give you the power to believe that the darkness is not as dark as it seems.

Holy and Loving God, you are eternal, and your vision
of the future is illuminated by wisdom and knowledge.
I am limited and finite.
Right now, the darkness seems to be my pervasive reality.
Help me to restore my hope in the future,
and guide me with your light. Amen.

PERSPECTIVE

You are the one who created my innermost parts;
you knit me together while I was still in my mother's womb.
—Psalm 139:13

Summertime arrived shortly after our divorce was final. I went to the store and returned armed with fresh food to grill. I set about prepping the meat and corncobs, plunked them on the tray to carry outside, and suddenly felt a jolt in my heart. I had no idea how to light the grill.

Staring at the food, raw and seasoned, I let the wave of loss wash over me. But, the kids were hungry and clamoring for dinner. There was nothing I could do except laugh at my own foolishness. After a quick online search and video tutorial, I learned how to use my own equipment. I grilled the food; it was delicious.

When you leave your family of origin to create a new family, it takes time to discover who you will be in the context of this new family system. If this system breaks down, you are left to find out who you are on your own. Nearly everyone experiences some confusion about who he or she is and to whom he or she belongs. Even if your divorce is amicable, it will take time to settle into your new identity as an unmarried person. The sense of belonging that you anticipated in your marriage is replaced with something new and unfamiliar. Still, remember that God is with you. You are never alone, and you will always belong to God. Even if your role shifts and changes, you will still be a beloved child of God.

Holy and Gracious God, you know me better than I know myself.
Help me to be gracious and kind while I'm learning how
to understand who I am and whose I am.
Thank you for never letting me go. Amen.

SINGLENESS

I give thanks to you that I was marvelously set apart.
Your works are wonderful—I know that very well.

—Psalm 139:14

When a marriage ends, your status as a person in partnered relationship suddenly expires. It is hard to adjust to being single, as your life has been built around shared experiences with another person. It will take time to come to terms with your singleness. The world seems to make a mockery of unmarried people, especially if they have children. There is the perpetual assumption of intact family units, which seems tragic and unfair.

If you are struggling with your singleness, give yourself the grace to adapt to your new status. Remember that it took time to build a relationship with your spouse, and you now have the opportunity to learn who you are as an individual all over again, which will also take time. Let Psalm 139 remind you that God created you *for you*, not for anyone else. You, beloved, are fearfully and wonderfully made. God made you, exactly as you are, with the understanding that your life, gifts, joys, talents, and uniqueness would change the world on your own terms. You don't need someone else in your life to validate your experiences. No one will *make* you happy; you will make your own joy. While you may have responsibilities to other people (such as children or coworkers) that must be fulfilled, you can focus on yourself. Show kindness to yourself—you are fearfully and wonderfully made.

Loving God, in your wisdom you have created me.
Thank you for all that I mean to others, to my friends and family.
I thank you for the love that abides to tie us all together.
Where you are, O God, there is love. Amen.

OWNERSHIP

My frame was not hidden from you,
when I was made in the secret place,
when I was woven together in the depths of the earth.
—Psalm 139:15

In the wake of divorce, you may find yourself swimming in an ocean of blame. Your heart will feel tender to the ways in which your spouse wronged or hurt you, so easy to identify now. Grievous wrongs in your relationship may have caused you to accept the divorce as a solution to toxic problems. Taking ownership of your situation doesn't mean validating your spouse's behavior. You are not responsible for infidelity or abuse, for example. You can seek to own the ways in which you participated in a broken system. Doing so will help you understand the creation and perpetuation of that system.

According to scripture, God knows your frame; when you were "woven in the depths of the earth," God saw and knew you. God understands who you are and how you got here. God loves you because of, and in spite of, your choices or mistakes. This is true for your spouse, as well. As you pray about what went wrong, give yourself the grace to acknowledge your failures as well. If you failed to love yourself enough to say no to an unhealthy partnership in the beginning, begin to care more for your heart. If you failed to keep your marriage covenant because you felt isolated or rejected, remember that the hurt you visited on your spouse didn't ease your pain. Your pain gives you the opportunity to love and care for yourself and to cope with failed expectations in healthier ways. Owning your role will help you lead a life filled with love in the future.

Holy and All-Knowing God,
you have known me since before my beginning.
You understand who I am, with all of my flaws and failings.
Help me to love myself, just as you love me. Amen.

LOVE

Your eyes saw my embryo,
and on your scroll every day was written
that was being formed for me,
before any one of them had yet happened.

—Psalm 139:16

What is love now that we have loved and lost? In my own marriage, I anticipated that my spouse could love me wholly and completely. I held the expectation that this person could provide for me the fullness of one emotion and that I could do the same in return. But, as marriage will teach you, spouses are flawed and broken people like us. Expecting you be the perfect model of unconditional love for each other was unfair to begin with. We all want our marriage to be better, healthier, more complete than other relationships we've had. And so, when the marriage is over, our vision of love is tarnished.

The psalmist writes of the sort of love our hearts yearn for: the sort of love that can know us completely, with all of our beauty and scars, and still love us fully. This is the sort of love we expected in our marriages. The beauty of this psalm is not only that God knows all of our days, but that God saw us as unformed, could envision our path, and offered us unconditional love on each step of our unfolding journey. What a gift to find this sort of love in our creator, who promises to love us now and always.

Holy and Loving God, help me to restore my faith in love.
You have loved me since before I was formed. You loved me
when you knew my marriage would fail, and you love me
into my new journey in life. Help me to receive your love,
so that I can learn how to love fully again. Amen.

ANNIVERSARY

How precious to me are your thoughts, God!
How vast is the sum of them!
—*Psalm 139:17 (NIV)*

It will happen once a year for the rest of your life: your wedding anniversary. If you are in the midst of the darkest part of your separation, then your anniversary will likely bear with it deep pain. Let it, for a moment. Let your marriage, with all of its good intentions, be the sole focus of your thoughts. As the psalmist writes of the weightiness of God's thoughts, the vastness of God's imagination, so can you permit your thoughts and feelings and memories of your marriage to press on you. Name your hurts. Cry your tears. Your pain is real and demands to be felt.

When you are ready, consider ways to reframe your anniversary. As you think back, are there parts of your marriage you can give thanks for? What have you gained through your marriage? What gifts has your divorce brought you? Even the loss of this intimate relationship can teach you compassion, patience, and gratitude. Your anniversary may not bring you joy this year, but it may feel different in the future. Even today, though, when your heart and thoughts are heavy, God is near to bear the weight of it all.

Loving and Gracious God,
thank you for being a God with whom
I can share my thoughts and who will receive my burdens.
Help me to see that when I share my burdens with you,
you can help them to become lighter. Amen.

DISAPPOINTMENT

If I tried to count [your thoughts, God]—
they outnumber grains of sand!
If I came to the very end—I'd still be with you.
—Psalm 139:18

When you plan a life together with someone, your thoughts become oriented completely around your coexistence, and separating those thoughts can be difficult. To some extent, you shared everything with another person: making a shopping list, organizing chores or responsibilities, managing your finances, and so on. Establishing a new way to think about your life means making space for new thoughts without your spouse in the center of them. This reorientation usually involves a profound sense of disappointment. After all, given the magnitude of hopes and dreams pinned on your union at your wedding, a failed marriage can be seen as the ultimate disappointment. Your head and your heart both created a vision of your future that will no longer be what you imagined. This disappointment can be crushing and overwhelming.

The psalmist writes about the immeasurable thoughts that God has about creation and all of her parts. "I come to the end," says the psalmist, "I am still with you." Even in the face of crushing disappointment, the psalmist reminds us that God will be our faithful and steadfast partner. It is our creator who made us, who cares for us, and who will sustain us in this season of change and reorientation. Today, let us give our disappointment over to God. Doing so makes room for new thoughts, not necessarily about your loss or failed expectations, but about the new things that are open to you. Even when you come to the end, God is with you. You are not alone.

Almighty and Powerful God, take my disappointment from me.
Help me see how loss makes new space for new growth,
as pruning roses allows them to blossom more fully. Amen.

REVENGE

If only, God, you would kill the wicked!
If only murderers would get away from me—
The people who talk about you, but only for wicked schemes.
—Psalm 139:19-20

Raising young children provides ample opportunity to witness humans' natural instinct to seek harm for harm done. When we are hurting, we naturally tend to want those who hurt us to hurt just as deeply. But this is revenge, not justice. In Psalm 139:19, the psalmist taps into this deep and dark feeling, asking for the wicked to be killed so that the psalmist's own suffering will end.

During my separation and divorce, I had days when I would pray for justice but would happily accept revenge in its place. At times, I prayed for the pendulum of sorrow to swing in the opposite direction because I was so deeply hurt. I wanted my attorney, the judge, and everyone I knew to see that the only way to right the wrongs I felt and heal my wounded heart was for the most perilous of penalties to befall my spouse. This didn't happen, and in the long run, I wouldn't have wanted it to. If my darkest prayers for revenge had been realized, my children would be brokenhearted. Even though I wanted revenge, I knew it wouldn't help anyone.

Almighty and Peaceful God, heal my heart,
that I might pray for justice
rather than revenge.
Give me grace that I may seek peace in my life
as we go our separate ways. Amen.

BETRAYAL

The people who are your enemies...
Use your name as if it were of no significance.

—*Psalm 139:20*

The words: "As long as we both shall live" are powerful. On my worst days, these words roll in my conscience with bitter longing. The one who vowed, publicly, to love me forever had left me for good. When you are betrayed by your beloved, the feelings are profound. You made eternal promises to one another, and put your whole trust in your broken selves to be able to keep these promises. Naturally, it will be hard to trust people and God again. If you're like me, you've prayed with fist-shaking rage more than once about God's role in the unfolding events. How dare you lead me to this person, God? How dare you allow my heart to soften so that I trusted him? How dare you let him hurt me like this!

The psalmist writes with very pointed language about those who speak against God maliciously, who lift themselves up for evil. I felt ashamed when I realized my prayers sounded malicious, as if God was to blame for my failed marriage. The truth is that people are rarely all good or all bad. We all exist on a spectrum of our best and worst selves. In order to heal from the feelings of betrayal, try to pray to release your spouse from his or her vows. Pray to release yourself from yours. Remember that it is God who is steadfast, faithful, and true. God is our model of a keeper of a promise to love and abide forever, not our former spouse or ourselves.

Gracious and Loving God, teach me your ways.
Show me how to be steadfast in my promise to be your disciple
and a loving example of grace and peace in the world.
Heal my heart, and set me free. Amen.

LOSS

Don't I hate everyone who hates you?
Don't I despise those who attack you?

—*Psalm 139:21*

Shortly after my divorce was final, I received an invitation to a friend's wedding. As expected, it was addressed only to me. My friend knew I'd be attending the ceremony and reception alone, and I felt a deep shame in my heart as I selected the filet mignon and sealed the response card. What a sad thing, I thought, to attend a wedding alone, after years of having a guaranteed name included alongside mine. For a moment, my sorrow overtook me and I felt a feeling as strong as hatred toward the happy couple, as if their joy was a condemnation of my own relationship's failing.

After a moment, I realized my foolishness. My quarrel was not with this couple at all. The sting of their joy didn't make them my enemies. There is not a finite amount of joy in the world, and someone else's happiness doesn't take away from your own. When someone finds love or happiness, do not begrudge them. Tend to your pain. Then celebrate with them. Delight that their joy can bring you joy. Be gracious. There is plenty of love and happiness to go around. Let us not allow bitterness to poison the ways in which the world is good. Our loss is not someone else's gain; our loss is what will open our eyes to the beautiful things that are happening all around us.

Almighty and Loving God, help my heart
when I turn toward anger and hatred.
Allow me the grace to experience loss
without resenting the happiness of others. Amen.

SHAME

Don't I despise those who attack you?
Yes, I hate them—through and through!
They've become my enemies too.

—*Psalm 139:21-22*

Perhaps you have days when hatred is easier to access than love. I had long stretches of time when I wanted to withdraw to a windowless room so that I could avoid any and all sentiments of happiness and joy. I wanted hatred alone to determine how I felt about other people, my former spouse, even myself. It took me a long time to realize that my hatred was born out of shame.

Society tells us that if we had it together, we'd be happily married to a financially stable spouse with 2.5 children and a well-trained pet. If we don't achieve this external metric of success, or if we lose it somehow, shame can easily creep into our bones and churn in our bellies. Shame is a clever emotion. While guilt tells us that we *did* something bad, shame sends us the more malignant message that we *are* bad. I felt catastrophic shame about my failed marriage. I feared my divorce had damaged me forever; I, and the new life that stretched before me, would never be whole.

But God promises again and again to stay with us, no matter how bad we think we are. God knows the pain of shame and is able to redeem it. Shame and hatred do not have to drive your thoughts or feelings; God's grace is great enough to restore you to wholeness and joy.

Powerful and Loving God, show me your grace.
Forgive me for what I have thought, said, and done.
Take my hatred and shame from me, leaving only my heart
as a vessel ready to receive and give love. Amen.

HOME

Search me, God, and know my heart;
test me and know my anxious thoughts.
—*Psalm 139:23 (NIV)*

One of the certainties of divorce is an address change. At least one of you will move from your marital home. If you stay in the home you share, it will change appreciably. When my spouse moved out, my heart was broken, and so was my home. I had trouble sleeping; I felt restless because home no longer felt like home.

One night I stopped fighting for sleep and admitted that I was awake and was going to stay that way. I took it upon myself to rearrange the furniture in the living room. And dining room. And kitchen. I sorted, organized, and replaced everything I could touch. By the end of the night, I was exhausted and empowered.

It was as if, hearing my thoughts and knowing the anxiety in my heart, God had whispered to me, "Make this your own." God nudged me to reorganize my space without consultation or negotiation. It was beautiful. It felt clean, welcoming, and peaceful. It took courage for me to acknowledge that my spouse wasn't returning, but making peace with this meant that I could build a home that reflected who I was. Home once again became the place where my heart was, and my heart was no longer restless.

Holy and Loving God,
know my thoughts, and guide me
on the path toward healing.
Know my heart, and hear its deepest longings.
Help my journey home,
that I might be able to create a new life
born out of your love and care. Amen.

GATEWAY TO FRIENDSHIP

See if there is any offensive way in me,
and lead me in the way everlasting.

—Psalm 139:24 (NIV)

When I was a child, my parents had a difficult marriage. It was confusing to me; I often didn't understand what was happening or if they would ever stop fighting. When I was eighteen, my parents divorced. I wasn't surprised, but I was heartbroken. That is, until I watched my parents became best friends and better parents divorced than they were married. Their discordant dynamic was no longer what defined them, and they allowed each other space to be better in every way—to themselves, each other, and to me.

As an adult, I prayed that my marriage would be healthy and long-lasting. My spouse and I tried mightily but could not resolve our differences. It took me a long time to realize that a healthy divorce could allow space for a healthier relationship. Since we share children, we will always be in one another's lives. I realize for some people, this is not the case and, in fact, some people need to isolate themselves from their former spouse for reasons of physical or emotional safety. But for those of us whose marriages were not good but not unsafe, divorce may be the very thing that helps us forge a healthy relationship with this other person we once knew so well.

Holy and Loving God, you have been the light in our darkness
and the hope in our loss. Remind us, each day,
that the worst thing is never the last thing,
and that new things are always possible.
We thank you for the wonderful and surprising ways
that you bless us, now and always. Amen.

NOTES

1. SHATTERED DREAMS AND HOPES

1. Paul Bohannan, *Divorce and After: An Analysis of the Social and Emotional Problems of Divorce* (Garden City, NY: Doubleday and Company, 1971).

2. IDENTITY CRISIS

1. Stephen R. Covey, *The 7 Habits of Highly Effective People: Powerful Lessons in Personal Change* (New York: Free Press, 2004), 109.

3. THE PATH FORWARD

1. E. Mavis Hetherington and John Kelly, *For Better or For Worse: Divorce Reconsidered* (New York: Norton, 2002), 5.

2. Hetherington and Kelly, 102.

3. Heatherington and Kelly, 103.

4. *The Simpsons*, season 22, episode 3, "MoneyBart," aired October 10, 2010, directed by Nancy Kruse, written by Tim Long.

4. TRAVELING WITH CHILDREN

1. E. Mavis Hetherington and John Kelly, *For Better or For Worse: Divorce Reconsidered* (New York: Norton, 2002), 110–23.

2. Heatherington and Kelly, 112.

3. Heatherington and Kelly, 112.

4. Heatherington and Kelly, 124–59.

5. SURVIVOR'S TOOL KIT

1. Stephen Ilardi, *The Depression Cure: The 6-Step Program to Beat Depression without Drugs* (Cambridge, MA: Da Capo Press, 2009).

2. Ilardi, 11.

3. Ilardi, 14.

4. Ilardi, 16.

5. Matthew Walker, *Why We Sleep: Unlocking the Power of Sleep and Dreams* (New York: Scribner, 2017).

6. E. Mavis Hetherington and John Kelly, *For Better or For Worse: Divorce Reconsidered* (New York: Norton, 2002), 108–9.

DEVOTIONS

1. Walter Brueggemann, *The Message of the Psalms: A Theological Commentary* (Minneapolis, MN: Fortress Press, 1984), 104.

2. Jane Hirshfield, "Hope and Love," in *The Lives of the Heart* (New York: Harper Collins, 1997).

CPSIA information can be obtained
at www.ICGtesting.com
Printed in the USA
LVHW090207230419
615136LV00001B/4/P

9 781501 881343